More
SILLY SIGNS

You will also enjoy:
Silly Signs

More
SILLY SIGNS

First Scholastic printing, November 1991

More
SILLY SIGNS

Compiled by Jeannette A. Fidell

Illustrated by Tom Funk

SCHOLASTIC INC.
New York Toronto London Auckland Sydney

ISBN 0-590-44837-4

12 11 10 9 8 7 6 5 4 3 2 1   1 2 3 4 5 6/9

Printed in the U.S.A.   01

First Scholastic printing, November 1991

Name of yogurt shop:
HUMPHREY YOGURT

Sign on bike shop:

CYCLE-LOGICAL

Sign in cabinetmaker's shop:
WOODEN IT BE NICE

Sign in barbershop:

JULIUS SCISSOR

Sign in glass store:

WE CURE YOUR WINDOWPANES.

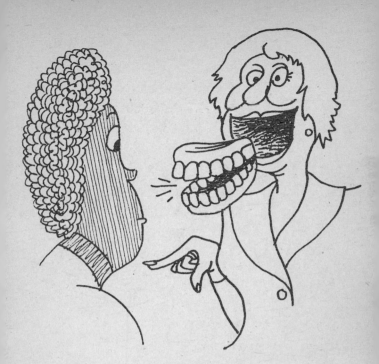

Sign in dentist's office:

**TELL YOUR FRIENDS ABOUT US.
IT'S ALL WORD OF MOUTH.**

Sign in long-established
dry cleaner's shop:

**THIRTY-EIGHT YEARS
ON THE SAME SPOT**

Lost and found ad:

LOST: $500 CASH
VALUE: $200

Name of restaurant:
LOVE & QUICHES

Sign in rod and reel store:

COME IN AND BE AN AFISHIANADO.

Sign in restaurant:

DOUGHNUTS ARE DUNK FOOD.

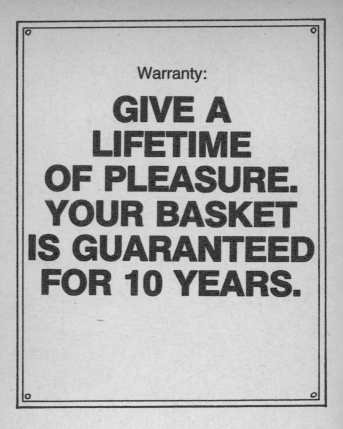

News item:

**PATIENT AT DEATH'S DOOR.
DOCTORS PULL HIM THROUGH.**

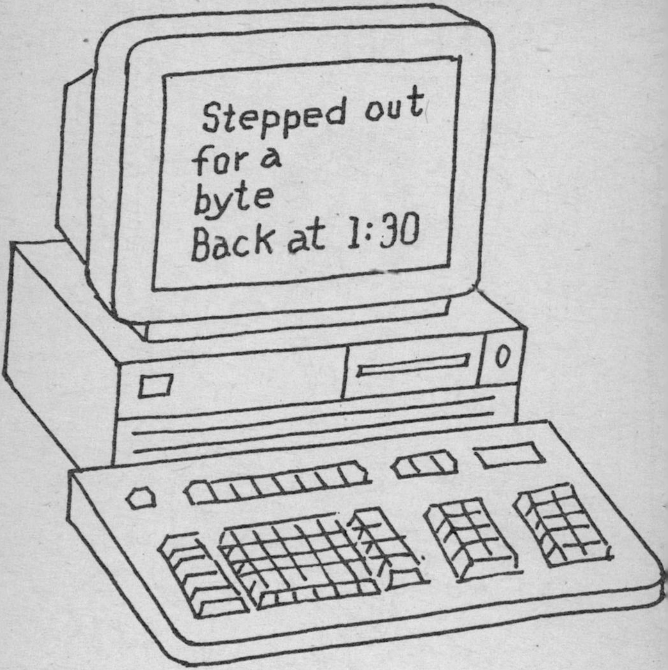
Stepped out
for a
byte
Back at 1:30

Newspaper headline:

MARCH PLANNED FOR NEXT AUGUST

I OWE, I OWE, SO OFF TO WORK I GO

Ad for sailing school:

ON THE JIB TRAINING

Sign in clothing store:

**STOP LIVING IN THE IRON AGE.
BUY PERMANENT PRESS.**

Sign in clock-repair shop:

**IF IT DOESN'T TICK,
TOCK TO US.**

Sign in delicatessen:

Sign in stationery store:

**SALE ON CALCULATORS.
LITTLE THINGS COUNT.**

Ad for bartender school:

OUR GRADUATES WILL WIND UP BEHIND BARS.

TV cable company ad:

LET
US
IMPROVE
YOUR
IMAGE.

Ad for clothing store:

**WONDERFUL BARGAINS FOR MEN
WITH 16 OR 17 NECKS.**

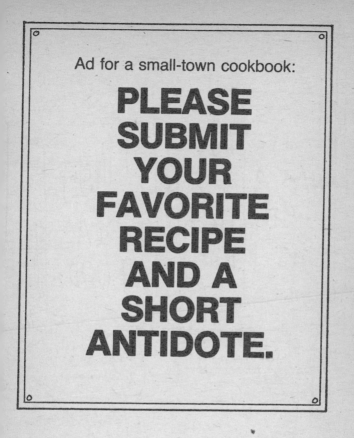

Ad for a small-town cookbook:

**PLEASE
SUBMIT
YOUR
FAVORITE
RECIPE
AND A
SHORT
ANTIDOTE.**

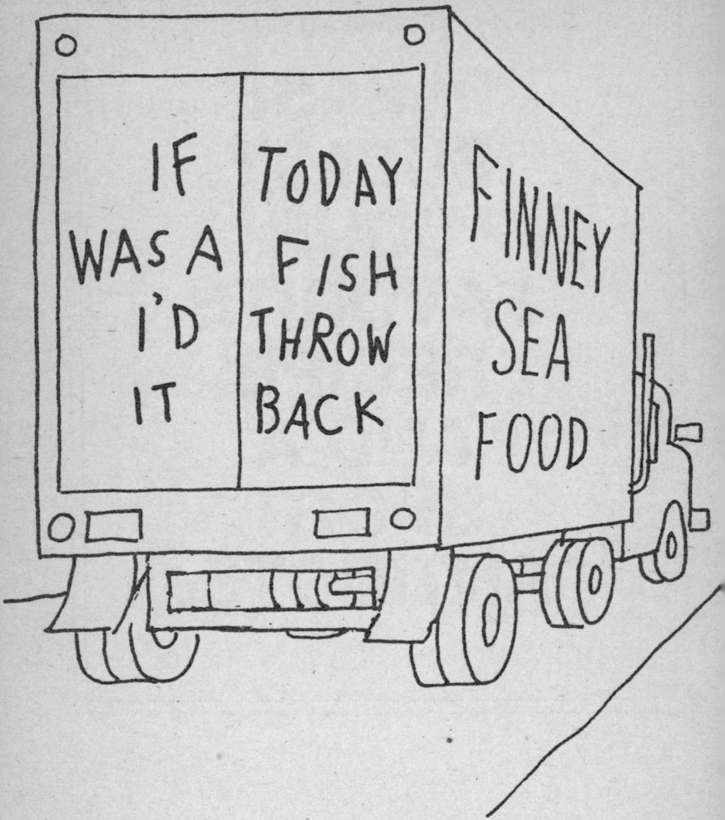
IF TODAY
WAS A FISH
I'D THROW
IT BACK
FINNEY
SEA
FOOD

Ad for a bank:

**MONEY TALKS! LISTEN UP.
BANK WITH US.**

Sign in bakery:

**OUR PIES SERVE FOUR HUNGRY
OR SIX POLITE PEOPLE.**

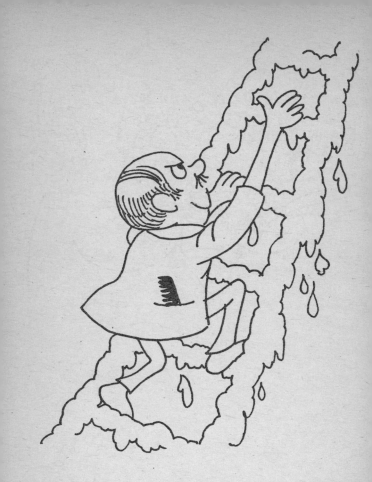

Sign in barbershop:

**WE CLIMBED THE LATHER
TO SUCCESS.**

Sign in grocery store:

OPEN
SEVEN DAYS
A WEEK
AND WEEKENDS.

HATS FOR ALL HEADS:
small
MEDIUM

Sign in dress shop during renovations:

PARDON US WHILE WE CHANGE INTO SOMETHING MORE COMFORTABLE.

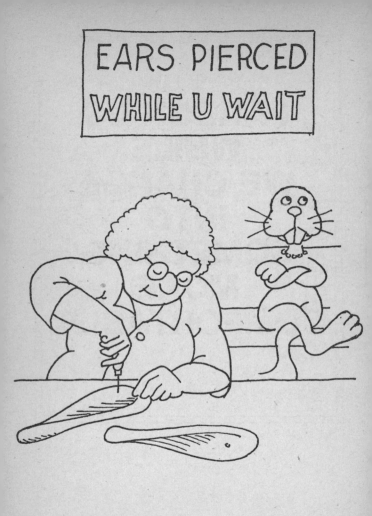

Ad in newspaper:

**TIRED OF CLEANING YOURSELF?
LET ME DO IT.**

Ad in newspaper:

**FOR SALE: ANTIQUE DESK
SUITABLE FOR LADY
WITH THICK LEGS**

Ad in newspaper:

**HELP WANTED:
MEN TO WORK
IN DYNAMITE FACTORY;
MUST BE WILLING TO TRAVEL**

Name of dress shop:

THE APPARELS
OF PAULINE

Sign in fishing-tackle store:

WE HAVE LIVE BAIT, DEAD BAIT, ARTIFICIAL BAIT, AND BAIT YOU CAN EAT IF THE FISH DON'T.

Sign in restaurant:

YES,
WE ARE OPEN.
SORRY
FOR THE
INCONVENIENCE.

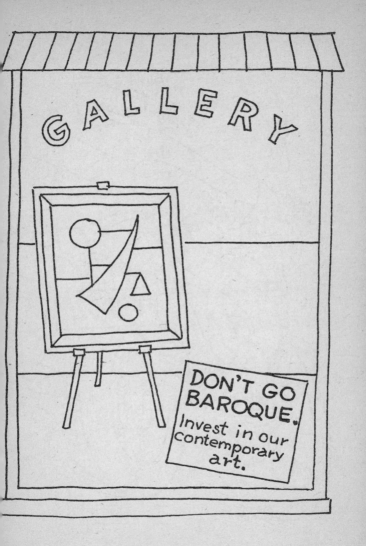

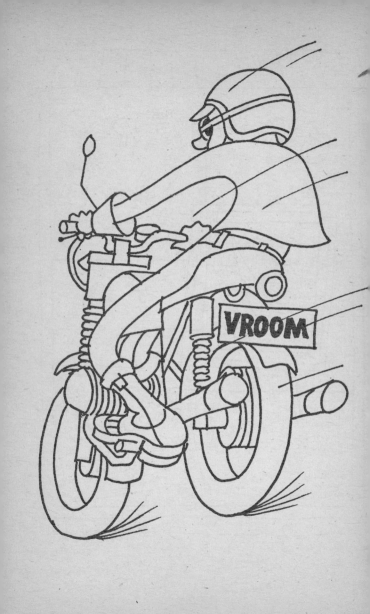